Copyright © 1992 by Gus Clarke
First published in Great Britain by Andersen Press Limited. All rights reserved. No part
of this book may be reproduced or utilized in any form or by any means, electronic or
mechanical, including photocopying and recording, or by any information storage and
retrieval system, without permission in writing from the Publisher. Inquiries should be
addressed to Lothrop, Lee & Shepard Books, a division of William Morrow & Company,
Inc., 1350 Avenue of the Americas, New York, New York 10019. Printed in Italy.

First U.S. Edition 1993
1 2 3 4 5 6 7 8 9 10

Library of Congress Cataloging in Publication Data was not available in time for
publication of this book, but can be obtained from the Library of Congress.
ISBN 0-688-12215-9
Library of Congress Catalog Card Number: 92-53462

the story of Old MacDonald, who had
a farm, with pictures by Gus Clarke.

Lothrop, Lee & Shepard Books
New York

For Emma, Ruth, and David

Old MacDonald had a farm,

And on that farm he had some...

Ducks

With a QUACK QUACK here and a QUACK QUACK there

Here a QUACK   there a QUACK

Everywhere a QUACK QUACK

Old MacDonald had a farm,

And on that farm he had some...

And on that farm he had some...

And on that farm he had some...

Hens

With a *CLUCK CLUCK* here and a *CLUCK CLUCK* there
Here a *CLUCK* there a *CLUCK*
Everywhere a *CLUCK CLUCK*

Old MacDonald had a farm,

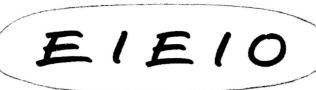

And on that farm he had some...

And on that farm he had some...

And on that farm he had some...

Now, on that farm he'd had...

And now he runs a...

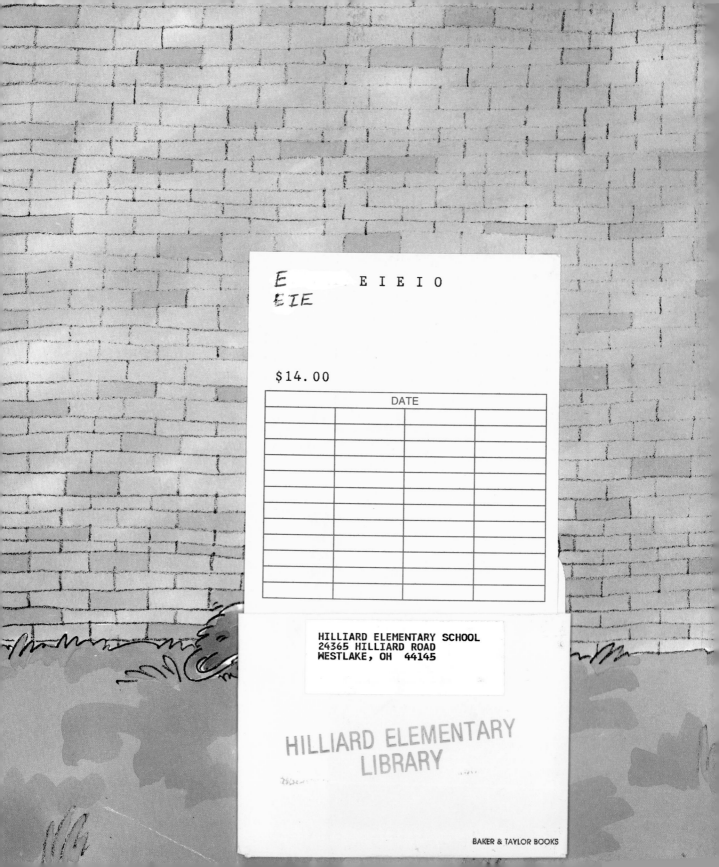

E I E I O
EIE

$14.00

DATE			

BAKER & TAYLOR BOOKS